MW01031845

THis WE BELIEVE

A Statement of Belief of the
Wisconsin Evangelical Lutheran Synod

Prepared for the Conference of Presidents by the
Commission on Inter-Church Relations for the
Wisconsin Evangelical Synod, 1999

Eleventh printing, 2007
Tenth printing, 2001
Revised, January 1999
Ninth printing, April 1988
Revised, September 1980
Sixth printing, May 1978
First printing, January 1967

Northwestern Publishing House
1250 N. 113th St., Milwaukee, WI 53226-3284
© 1999 by Northwestern Publishing House
Published 1999
Printed in the United States of America
ISBN 978-0-8100-0983-7

INTRODUCTION

"Whoever acknowledges me before men, I will also acknowledge him before my Father in heaven" (Matthew 10:32). With these words Jesus indicates that he wants Christians to confess publicly what they believe in their hearts.

This We Believe is one way the members of the Wisconsin Evangelical Lutheran Synod have chosen to confess their faith in Christ. This document publicly summarizes the main teachings of our church body.

This We Believe was first published in 1967. A minor revision was undertaken in 1980. In consultation with the Conference of Presidents, the Commission on Inter-Church Relations completed the present revision in 1999. This second revision seeks to simplify the language and to add some important points of doctrine not addressed in the first two editions. The current revision was not undertaken because of doctrinal disagreement with the previous editions.

The current document does not claim to be a full treatment of all the Bible's teachings. For a fuller exposition of the doctrines of Scripture, the reader is referred to other sources, including the pamphlet *Doctrinal Statements of the WELS* (Northwestern Publishing House, 1997).

It should also be noted that *This We Believe* was not specifically designed to serve as an outreach tool for unchurched people, but as a basis for doctrinal discussions with other church bodies and informed individuals.

It is our conviction that over the years *This We Believe* has been a great blessing to the church. This revised edition is presented with the fervent prayer that it may continue to serve Christ's church, to the glory of his name and for the extension of his kingdom.

I. GOD AND HIS REVELATION

1. We believe that there is only one true God (Isaiah 44:6). He has made himself known as the triune God, one God in three persons. This is evident from Jesus' command to his disciples to baptize "in the name of the Father and of the Son and of the Holy Spirit" (Matthew 28:19). Whoever does not worship this God worships a false god, a god who does not exist. Jesus said, "He who does not honor the Son does not honor the Father, who sent him" (John 5:23).

2. We believe that God has revealed himself in nature. "The heavens declare the glory of God; the skies proclaim the work of his hands" (Psalm 19:1). "Since the creation of the world God's invisible qualities—his eternal power and divine nature—have been clearly seen, being understood from what has been made, so that men are without excuse" (Romans 1:20). So there is no excuse for atheists. Since the requirements of the law are written on people's hearts, the consciences of people also bear witness that there is a God to whom they are accountable (Romans 2:15). However, nature and conscience present only a partial revelation of God and one that is not able to show the way to heaven.

3. We believe that God has given the full revelation of himself in his Son, the Lord Jesus Christ. "No one has ever seen God, but God the One and Only, who is at the Father's side, has made him known" (John 1:18). In Jesus, God has revealed himself as the Savior-God, who "so loved the world

that he gave his one and only Son, that whoever believes in him shall not perish but have eternal life" (John 3:16).

4. We believe that God has also given a written revelation for all people in the Holy Scriptures. His revelation in the Bible has two main messages, the law and the gospel. The law declares what is right and wrong, and it threatens God's punishment for sin. The gospel presents the love of God, which he has shown especially by providing salvation from sin through Jesus Christ.

5. We believe that the entire Bible is Christ-centered. In the Old Testament God repeatedly promised a divine deliverer from sin, death, and hell. The New Testament proclaims that this promised deliverer has come in the person of Jesus of Nazareth. Jesus himself says of the Old Testament, "These are the Scriptures that testify about me" (John 5:39).

6. We believe that God gave the Scriptures through men whom he chose, using the language they knew and the style of writing they had. He used Moses and the prophets to write the Old Testament in Hebrew (some portions in Aramaic) and the evangelists and apostles to write the New Testament in Greek.

7. We believe that in a miraculous way that goes beyond all human investigation, God the Holy Spirit moved these men to write his Word. These men "spoke from God as they were carried along by the Holy Spirit" (2 Peter 1:21). What they said was spoken "not in words taught us by human wisdom but in words taught by the Spirit" (1 Corinthians 2:13). Every thought they expressed and every word they used were given them by the Holy Spirit. Saint Paul wrote to Timothy, "All Scripture is God-breathed" (2 Timothy 3:16).

The church has called this miraculous process *inspiration*, which means "breathing into." Since every word of Scripture was inspired, we also call this process verbal inspiration, or word-for-word inspiration. This is not to be equated with mechanical dictation, since the Holy Spirit guided the writers as they used their individual vocabularies and writing styles.

8. We believe that Scripture is a unified whole, true and without error in everything it says, for the Savior said, "The Scripture cannot be broken" (John 10:35). Therefore it is the infallible authority and guide for everything we believe and do.

9. We believe that the Bible is fully sufficient, clearly teaching people all they need to know to get to heaven. It makes them "wise for salvation through faith in Christ Jesus" (2 Timothy 3:15), and it equips them for "every good work" (2 Timothy 3:17). Since God's plan of salvation has been fully revealed in the canonical books of the Bible, we need and expect no other revelations (Hebrews 1:1,2). The church is built on the teachings of the apostles and prophets (Ephesians 2:20).

10. We believe and accept the Bible on its own terms, accepting as factual history what it presents as history and recognizing as figurative speech what is evident as such. We believe that Scripture must interpret Scripture, clear passages throwing light on those less easily understood. We believe that no authority—whether it is human reason, science, or scholarship—may stand in judgment over Scripture. Sound scholarship will faithfully search out the true meaning of Scripture without presuming to pass judgment on it.

11. We believe that the original Hebrew text of the Old Testament and the Greek text of the New Testament are the inspired Word of God. Translations of the Hebrew and Greek that accurately reflect the meaning of the original text convey God's truth to people and can properly be called the Word of God.

12. Although the original documents themselves have been lost, we believe that the Lord in his providential care has accurately preserved the Hebrew and Greek texts through the many hand-copied manuscripts that exist. Although there are minor differences or "variants" between the various hand-copied manuscripts, these variants do not cause any changes in doctrine.

13. We believe that the three ecumenical creeds (the Apostles', the Nicene, and the Athanasian) as well as the Lutheran Confessions as contained in the Book of Concord of 1580 express the true doctrine of Scripture. Since the doctrines they confess are drawn from Scripture alone, we are bound to them in our faith and life. Therefore all preaching and teaching in our churches and schools must be in harmony with these confessions, and we reject all the errors that they reject.

14. We reject any worship that is not directed to the triune God as revealed in the Bible. We reject the use of feminine names and pronouns for God because in Scripture God reveals himself as Father and Son. We reject the opinion that all religions lead to the same God.

15. We reject any thought that makes only part of Scripture God's Word or that allows for the possibility of factual error in Scripture, even in so-called nonreligious matters such as historical or geographical details. We

likewise reject all views that say Scripture is merely a human record of God's revelation as he encounters mankind in history, and so is a record subject to human imperfections.

16. We reject any emphasis upon Jesus as the personal Word of God (John 1:1) that minimizes the role of the Scriptures as the written Word of God (Romans 3:2).

17. We reject every effort to reduce the confessions contained in the Book of Concord to historical documents that do not have binding confessional significance for the church today. We likewise reject any claim that the church is bound only to those doctrines of Scripture that are specifically addressed in these confessions.

This is what Scripture teaches about God and his revelation. This we believe, teach, and confess.

II. CREATION, MANKIND, AND SIN

1. We believe that the universe, the world, and the human race came into existence in the beginning when God created heaven and earth and all creatures (Genesis 1,2). Further testimony to this event is found in other passages of the Old and New Testaments (for example, Exodus 20:11; Hebrews 11:3). The creation happened in the course of six consecutive days of normal length by the power of God's almighty word.

2. We believe that the Bible presents a true, factual, and historical account of creation.

3. We believe that God created Adam and Eve in his own image (Genesis 1:26,27), that is, holy and righteous. Their thoughts, desires, and will were in full harmony with God (Colossians 3:10; Ephesians 4:24). They were furthermore given the capacity to "subdue" God's creation (Genesis 1:28) and the responsibility to care for it (Genesis 2:15).

4. We believe that God created a multitude of good angels. Sometime after creation, a number of these angels rebelled against God under the leadership of one of their own who is called Satan or the devil (2 Peter 2:4). Ever since, these evil angels have opposed God and God's people (1 Peter 5:8).

5. We believe that Adam and Eve lost their divine image when they yielded to the temptation of Satan and disobeyed God's command. This brought upon them the

judgment of God: "You will surely die" (Genesis 2:17). Since that time all people are conceived and born in a sinful condition (Psalm 51:5) and are inclined only to evil (Genesis 8:21). "Flesh gives birth to flesh" (John 3:6). Since all people are by nature dead in sin and separated from God (Ephesians 2:1), they are unable to reconcile themselves to God by their own efforts and deeds.

6. We believe that God in his gracious providence richly and daily provides for the bodily needs of all people (Psalm 145:15,16). He furthermore protects believers against all danger by keeping evil away from them (Psalm 121:7) or by making it serve their good (Romans 8:28).

7. We reject all theories of evolution as an explanation of the origin of the universe and the human race and all attempts to harmonize the scriptural account of creation with such theories.

8. We reject interpretations that reduce the first chapters of Genesis to a narration of myths or parables or poetic accounts that are not factual history.

9. We reject all theories that blur the distinction between human beings and animals, since only human beings have immortal souls and are accountable to God.

10. We reject all theories that blur the distinction between God and his creation (pantheism).

11. We reject all views that look upon people as basically good by nature; that consider their natural tendencies to be mere weaknesses, which are not sinful; or that fail to recognize their total spiritual depravity and their inability to please God (Romans 3:9-18).

This is what Scripture teaches about creation, mankind, and sin. This we believe, teach, and confess.

III. CHRIST AND REDEMPTION

1. We believe that Jesus Christ is the eternal Son of God, one with the Father from all eternity (John 1:1,2). In the course of time, he took a true and complete, yet sinless, human nature to himself (Galatians 4:4) when he was conceived as a holy child in the virgin Mary through a miracle of the Holy Spirit (Luke 1:35). God's angel testified, "What is conceived in her is from the Holy Spirit" (Matthew 1:20). Jesus Christ is unique, for in him the true God and a true human nature are inseparably united in one person, the holy God-man. He is called Immanuel, which means "God with us" (Matthew 1:23).

2. We believe that Jesus at all times possessed the fullness of the Deity with all divine power, wisdom, and glory (Colossians 2:9). His divinity was evident when he performed miracles (John 2:11). But while he lived on earth, he took on the form of a servant, humbling himself by laying aside the continuous and full display and use of his divine characteristics. During this time he lived as a man among mankind, endured suffering, and humbled himself to the shameful death on the cross (Philippians 2:7,8). We believe that Christ descended into hell to proclaim his victory over Satan (1 Peter 3:18,19). We believe that he rose again from the grave with a glorified body, ascended, and is exalted on high to rule with power over the world, with grace in his church, and with glory in eternity (Philippians 2:9-11).

3. We believe that Jesus Christ, the God-man, was sent by the Father to redeem all people, that is, to buy them back from the guilt and punishment of sin. Jesus came to fulfill the law (Matthew 5:17) so that on the basis of his perfect obedience all people would be declared holy (Romans 5:18,19). He came to bear "the iniquity of us all" (Isaiah 53:6), ransoming all people by his sacrifice for sin on the altar of the cross (Matthew 20:28). We believe that he is the God-appointed substitute for all people. His righteousness, or perfect obedience, is accepted by the Father as our righteousness, his death for sin as our death for sin (2 Corinthians 5:21). We believe that his resurrection gives full assurance that God has accepted the payment he made for all (Romans 4:25).

4. We believe that God reconciled "the world to himself in Christ, not counting men's sins against them" (2 Corinthians 5:19). We believe that Jesus is "the Lamb of God, who takes away the sin of the world" (John 1:29). The mercy and grace of God are all-embracing; the reconciliation through Christ is universal; the forgiveness of sins has been gained as an accomplished fact for all people. Because of the substitutionary work of Christ, God has justified all people, that is, God has declared them to be not guilty. This forms the firm, objective basis for the sinner's assurance of salvation.

5. We reject any teaching that in any way limits Christ's work of atonement. We reject any teaching that says Christ paid the penalty only for the sins of some people. We reject any teaching that says Christ made only a partial payment for sins.

6. We reject the views that consider the Gospel accounts to be pious fiction developed by early Christians

to express their ideas about Jesus Christ rather than a true account of what actually happened in history. We reject all attempts to make the historical accuracy of events in Christ's life—such as his virgin birth, his miracles, or his bodily resurrection—appear unimportant or even doubtful. We reject the attempts to stress a "present encounter with the living Christ" in such a way that Jesus' redemptive work recorded in Scripture loses its importance.

This is what Scripture teaches about Christ and redemption. This we believe, teach, and confess.

IV. JUSTIFICATION BY GRACE THROUGH FAITH

1. We believe that God has justified all sinners, that is, he has declared them righteous for the sake of Christ. This is the central message of Scripture upon which the very existence of the church depends. It is a message relevant to people of all times and places, of all races and social levels, for "the result of one trespass was condemnation for all men" (Romans 5:18). All need forgiveness of sins before God, and Scripture proclaims that all have been justified, for "the result of one act of righteousness was justification that brings life for all men" (Romans 5:18).

2. We believe that individuals receive this free gift of forgiveness not on the basis of their own works, but only through faith (Ephesians 2:8,9). Justifying faith is trust in Christ and his redemptive work. This faith justifies not because of any power it has in itself, but only because of the salvation prepared by God in Christ, which it embraces (Romans 3:28; 4:5). On the other hand, although Jesus died for all, Scripture says that "whoever does not believe will be condemned" (Mark 16:16). Unbelievers forfeit the forgiveness won for them by Christ (John 8:24).

3. We believe that people cannot produce this justifying faith, or trust, in their own hearts, because "the man without the Spirit does not accept the things that come from the Spirit of God, for they are foolishness to him" (1 Corinthians 2:14). In fact, "the sinful mind is hostile to

God" (Romans 8:7). It is the Holy Spirit who gives people faith to recognize that "Jesus is Lord" (1 Corinthians 12:3). The Holy Spirit works this faith by means of the gospel (Romans 10:17). We believe, therefore, that a person's conversion is entirely the work of God's grace. Rejection of the gospel is, however, entirely the unbeliever's own fault (Matthew 23:37).

4. We believe that sinners are saved by grace alone. Grace is the undeserved love of God for sinners. This love led God to give sinners everything they need for their salvation. It is all a gift of God. People do nothing to earn any of it (Ephesians 2:8,9).

5. We believe that already before the world was created, God chose those individuals whom he would in time convert through the gospel of Christ and preserve in faith to eternal life (Ephesians 1:4-6; Romans 8:29,30). This election to faith and salvation in no way was caused by anything in people but shows how completely salvation is by grace alone (Romans 11:5,6).

6. We believe that at the moment of death, the souls of those who believe in Christ go immediately to be with the Lord in the joy of heaven because of the atoning work of Christ (Luke 23:43). The souls of those who do not believe in Christ go to an eternity of misery in hell (Luke 16:22-24).

7. We reject every teaching that people in any way contribute to their salvation. We reject the belief that people with their own power can cooperate in their conversion or make a decision for Christ (John 15:16). We reject the belief that those who are converted were less resistant to God's grace than those who remain unconverted. We reject all efforts to present faith as a condition people

must fulfill to complete their justification. We reject all attempts of sinners to justify themselves before God.

8. We reject any suggestion that the doctrine of justification by faith is no longer meaningful today.

9. We reject the teaching that believers can never fall from faith ("once saved, always saved"), because the Bible says it is possible for believers to fall from faith (1 Corinthians 10:12).

10. We reject the false and blasphemous conclusion that those who are lost were predestined, or elected, by God to damnation, for God wants all people to be saved (1 Timothy 2:4; 2 Peter 3:9).

11. We reject universalism, the belief that all people are saved, even those without faith in Christ (John 3:36). We reject pluralism, the belief that there are other ways to salvation besides faith in Christ (John 14:6; Acts 4:12). We reject any teaching that says it does not matter what one believes so long as one has faith in God.

This is what Scripture teaches about justification by grace through faith. This we believe, teach, and confess.

V. GOOD WORKS AND PRAYER

1. We believe that faith in Jesus Christ always leads a believer to produce works that are pleasing to God. "Faith by itself, if it is not accompanied by action, is dead" (James 2:17). As a branch in Christ the vine, a Christian produces good fruit (John 15:5).

2. We believe that works pleasing to God are works of love, for "love is the fulfillment of the law" (Romans 13:10). Faith, however, does not set up its own standards to determine what is loving (Matthew 15:9). True faith delights to do only what agrees with God's holy will. That will of God is revealed in the Bible, particularly in the Ten Commandments as their content is repeated in the New Testament. In wrestling with current moral problems, the Christian will therefore seek answers from God's law.

3. We believe, for example, that the Fifth Commandment teaches that all human life is a gift from God. This commandment speaks against abortion, suicide, and euthanasia ("mercy killing").

4. We believe that the Sixth Commandment regulates marriage and the family. God instituted marriage as a lifelong union of one man and one woman (Matthew 19:4-6). It is the only proper context for sexual intimacy and the procreation of children. A marriage can be ended without sin only when God ends the marriage through the death of one of the spouses. Nevertheless, a Christian may

obtain a divorce if his or her spouse has broken the marriage through adultery (Matthew 19:9) or malicious desertion (1 Corinthians 7:15). The Sixth Commandment forbids all sexual intimacy apart from marriage, including homosexuality (1 Corinthians 6:9,10).

5. We believe that individuals are free to make their own decisions concerning matters that are neither forbidden nor commanded by God's Word (adiaphora). People must be careful, however, that their use of this freedom does not cause others to sin.

6. We believe that good works, which are fruits of faith, must be distinguished from works of civic righteousness performed by unbelievers. Although unbelievers may do much that appears to be good and upright, these works are not good in God's sight, for "without faith it is impossible to please God" (Hebrews 11:6). While we recognize the value of such works for human society, we know that unbelievers cannot do their duty to God through works of civic righteousness.

7. We believe that in this world even the best works of Christians are tainted with sin. A sinful nature still afflicts every Christian. Therefore Christians often fail to do the good they want to do but keep on doing the evil they do not want to do (Romans 7:18-21). They must confess that all their righteous acts are like filthy rags (Isaiah 64:6). Because of Christ's redemption, however, these imperfect efforts of Christians are considered holy and acceptable by their heavenly Father.

8. We believe that the Holy Spirit enables every believer to produce good works as fruits of faith (Galatians 5:22-25). The Holy Spirit gives every believer a new

nature, or "new man," that cooperates with the Holy Spirit in doing good works. The Holy Spirit uses the gospel to motivate believers to do good works.

9. The Holy Spirit also equips the church with all the spiritual gifts it needs for its well-being (1 Corinthians 12:4-11). During the beginning of the New Testament era, special charismatic gifts were given to the church, such as signs, miracles, and speaking in tongues. These gifts were connected with the ministry of the apostles (2 Corinthians 12:12). There is no evidence in Scripture that we today should expect the continuation of such charismatic gifts.

10. We believe that a life of prayer is a fruit of faith. Confidently, through faith in their Savior, Christians address their heavenly Father with petitions and praise. They present their needs and the needs of others, and they give thanks (1 Timothy 2:1). Such prayers are a delight to God, and he grants their requests according to his wisdom (Matthew 7:7,8; 1 John 5:14).

11. We reject every thought that the good works of Christians in any way earn or contribute toward establishing a right relationship with God and gaining salvation in heaven.

12. We reject every attempt to abolish the unchanging moral law of God as revealed in the Bible as the absolute standard of what is right and wrong.

13. We reject the view that people may decide for themselves what is right and wrong apart from God's Word. We reject any misuse of the term *love* to condone behavior contrary to God's Word. We recognize these arguments as schemes of Satan to obscure the knowledge of God's holy will and to undermine the consciousness of sin.

14. We reject any view that considers the act of praying a means of grace. Although God certainly gives good gifts to believers in answer to their prayers, he conveys his forgiving grace and strengthens faith only through the Word and sacraments. Furthermore, we reject any view that looks upon prayer as beneficial only because it helps the one who prays feel better.

15. We reject the view that all prayers are acceptable to God, and we hold that the prayers of all who do not have faith in Christ are vain babbling addressed to false gods (Matthew 6:7).

This is what Scripture teaches about good works and prayer. This we believe, teach, and confess.

VI. THE MEANS OF GRACE

1. We believe that God bestows all spiritual blessings upon sinners by special means established by him. These are the means of grace, the gospel in Word and sacraments. We define a sacrament as a sacred act established by Christ in which the Word connected with an earthly element gives the forgiveness of sins.

2. We believe that through the gospel, the good news of Christ's atoning sacrifice for sinners, the Holy Spirit works faith in people, whose hearts are by nature hostile to God (1 Peter 1:23). Scripture teaches that "faith comes from hearing the message, and the message is heard through the word of Christ" (Romans 10:17). This Spirit-worked faith brings about a renewal in sinners and makes them heirs of eternal life in heaven.

3. We believe that also through the Sacrament of Baptism the Holy Spirit applies the gospel to sinners, giving them new life (Titus 3:5) and cleansing them from all sin (Acts 2:38). The Lord points to the blessing of Baptism when he promises, "Whoever believes and is baptized will be saved" (Mark 16:16). We believe that the blessing of Baptism is meant for all people (Matthew 28:19), including infants. Infants are born sinful (John 3:6) and therefore need to be born again, that is, to be brought to faith, through Baptism (John 3:5).

4. We believe that all who join in the Sacrament of the Lord's Supper receive the true body and blood of Christ in,

with, and under the bread and wine (1 Corinthians 10:16). This is true because, when the Lord instituted this sacrament, he said, "This is my body. This is my blood of the covenant, which is poured out for many for the forgiveness of sins" (Matthew 26:26,28). We believe that Christ's words of institution cause the real presence—not any human action. As believers receive his body and blood, they also receive the forgiveness of sins (Matthew 26:28) and the comfort and assurance that they are truly his own. Unbelievers also receive Christ's body and blood, but to their judgment (1 Corinthians 11:29).

5. We believe that the Lord gave his Word and the sacraments of Baptism and the Lord's Supper for a purpose. He commanded his followers, "Go and make disciples of all nations, baptizing them in the name of the Father and of the Son and of the Holy Spirit, and teaching them to obey everything I have commanded you" (Matthew 28:19,20). Through God's Word and sacraments he preserves and extends the holy Christian church throughout the world. Believers should therefore be diligent and faithful in the use of these divinely established means of grace for themselves and in their mission outreach to others. These are the only means through which immortal souls are brought to faith and to life in heaven.

6. We reject any views that look for the revelation of the grace of God and salvation apart from the gospel as found in the Scriptures. We reject any views that look for the Holy Spirit to work faith apart from the means of grace. We likewise reject the view that the law is a means of grace.

7. We reject the view that babies should not be baptized and that they cannot believe in Christ (Luke 18:15-17). We reject the view that baptism must be by immersion.

8. We reject all teachings that the Sacrament of the Altar offers nothing more than signs and symbols of Jesus' sacrifice, thereby denying that Christ's true body and blood are received in the Lord's Supper. We reject the view that those who eat the body of Christ in the sacrament merely receive Christ spiritually by faith. We reject the claim that unbelievers and hypocrites do not receive the true body and blood of Jesus in the Sacrament.

9. We reject the doctrine of transubstantiation, which teaches that the substance of the bread and wine are changed entirely into the body and blood of Christ. Scripture teaches that all communicants receive both the bread and wine and the body and blood of Christ (1 Corinthians 10:16).

10. We reject any attempt to set the precise moment within the celebration of the Lord's Supper when the body and blood of Christ become present. We therefore reject the view that one must believe that Christ's body and blood are present as soon as the words of consecration have been spoken and the view that one must believe that Christ's body and blood become present only at the moment of eating and drinking.

This is what Scripture teaches about the means of grace. This we believe, teach, and confess.

VII. CHURCH AND MINISTRY

1. We believe that there is one holy Christian church, which is the temple of God (1 Corinthians 3:16) and the body of Christ (Ephesians 1:23; 4:12). The members of this one church are all those who are the "sons of God through faith in Christ Jesus" (Galatians 3:26). The church, then, consists only of believers, or saints, whom God accepts as holy for the sake of Jesus' righteousness, which has been credited to them (2 Corinthians 5:21). These saints are scattered throughout the world. All people who believe that Jesus is their Savior from sin are members of the holy Christian church, regardless of the nation, race, or church body to which they belong.

2. We believe that this holy Christian church is a reality, although it is not an external, visible organization. Because "man looks at the outward appearance, but the LORD looks at the heart" (1 Samuel 16:7), only the Lord knows "those who are his" (2 Timothy 2:19). The members of the holy Christian church are known only to God; we cannot distinguish between true believers and hypocrites. The holy Christian church is therefore invisible and cannot be identified with any one church body or with the total membership of all church bodies.

3. We believe that the presence of the holy Christian church nevertheless can be recognized. Wherever the gospel is preached and the sacraments are administered, the holy Christian church is present, for through the

means of grace true faith is produced and preserved (Isaiah 55:10,11). The means of grace, therefore, are called the marks of the church.

4. We believe that it is the Lord's will that Christians meet regularly to build one another up by using the means of grace together (Hebrews 10:24,25) and to work for the spread of the gospel into all the world (Mark 16:15). Since these visible gatherings (for example, congregations and synods) use the means of grace, they are called churches. They bear this name, however, only because of the true believers present in them (1 Corinthians 1:2).

5. We believe that God directs believers to acknowledge oneness in faith with Christians whose confession of faith submits to all the teachings of Scripture (John 8:31; 1 Thessalonians 5:21,22). We believe, furthermore, that individuals through their membership in a church body commit themselves to the doctrine and practice of that church. To assert that unity exists where there is no agreement in confession is to presume to look into people's hearts. Only God can look into people's hearts. It is not necessary that all Christians agree on matters of church ritual or organization. About these the New Testament gives no commands (Romans 14:17).

6. We believe that those whose confession of faith reveals that they are united in the doctrines of Scripture will express their fellowship in Christ as occasion permits (Ephesians 4:3). They may express their fellowship by joint worship, by joint proclamation of the gospel, by joining in Holy Communion, by joint prayer, and by joint church work. God directs believers not to practice religious fellowship with those whose confession and actions reveal

that they teach, tolerate, support, or defend error (2 John 10,11). When error appears in the church, Christians will try to preserve their fellowship by patiently admonishing the offenders, in the hope that they will turn from their error (2 Timothy 2:25,26; Titus 3:10). But the Lord commands believers not to practice church fellowship with people who persist in teaching or adhering to beliefs that are false (Romans 16:17,18).

7. We believe that every Christian is a priest before God (1 Peter 2:9). All believers have direct and equal access to the throne of grace through Christ, the mediator (Ephesians 2:17,18). God has given the means of grace to all believers. All Christians are to declare the praises of him who called them out of darkness into his wonderful light (1 Peter 2:9). In this sense all Christians are ministers, or servants, of the gospel. God wants all Christians to share the message of salvation with other people (Matthew 28:19,20; 10:32).

8. We believe that God has also established the public ministry of the Word (Ephesians 4:11), and it is the will of God that the church, in accordance with good order (1 Corinthians 14:40), call qualified individuals into this public ministry (1 Timothy 3:1-10; 1 Corinthians 9:14). Such individuals minister publicly, that is, not because as individuals they possess the universal priesthood but because they are asked to do this in the name of fellow Christians (Romans 10:15). These individuals are the called servants of Christ and ministers of the gospel. They are not to be lords over God's church (1 Peter 5:3). We believe that when the church calls individuals into this public ministry, the Lord himself is acting through the church (Acts 20:28). We believe that the church has the

freedom to establish various forms within the one ministry of the Word, such as pastors, Christian teachers, and staff ministers. Through its call, the church in Christian liberty designates the place and scope of service.

9. We believe that the church's mission is to serve people with the Word and sacraments. This service is usually done in local congregations. We look upon the pastoral office as the most comprehensive form of the public ministry of the Word. Pastors are trained and called to provide such comprehensive spiritual oversight for the gathering and nurturing of souls in congregations (1 Peter 5:2).

10. We believe that women may participate in offices and activities of the public ministry except where that work involves authority over men (1 Timothy 2:11,12). This means that women may not serve as pastors nor participate in assemblies of the church in ways that exercise authority over men (1 Corinthians 11:3; 14:33-35).

11. We reject any attempt to identify the holy Christian church with an outward organization. We reject any claim that the church must function in the world through specific organizational forms.

12. We reject as false ecumenicity any views that look for the true unity of the church in some form of external or organizational union, and we oppose all movements toward such union made at the expense of a clear confession of all the teachings of Scripture. We reject the contention that religious fellowship may be practiced without agreement in doctrine and practice. There must be agreement in the confession of scriptural doctrines, and also one's actions or practice must show that error is not tolerated.

13. We reject participation or membership in organizations that have religious features in conflict with the Christian faith, such as most lodges.

This is what Scripture teaches about church and ministry. This we believe, teach, and confess.

VIII. CHURCH AND STATE

1. We believe that not only the church but also the state, that is, all governmental authority, has been instituted by God. "The authorities that exist have been established by God" (Romans 13:1). Christians will, therefore, for conscience' sake obey the government that rules over them (Romans 13:5) unless that government commands them to disobey God (Acts 5:29).

2. We believe that God has given the church and the state their own distinct responsibilities. To the church the Lord has assigned the responsibility of calling sinners to repentance, of proclaiming forgiveness through the cross of Christ, and of encouraging believers in their Christian living. The purpose is to lead the elect of God to eternal salvation through faith in Christ. To the state the Lord has assigned the duty of keeping good order and peace, of punishing the wrongdoer, and of arranging all civil matters in society (Romans 13:3,4). The purpose is "that we may live peaceful and quiet lives in all godliness and holiness" (1 Timothy 2:2).

3. We believe that the only means God has given to the church to carry out its assigned purpose are the Word and sacraments (Matthew 28:19,20). People are converted by the Holy Spirit only through the message of law and gospel, sin and grace, the wrath of God against sin and the mercy of God in Christ. We believe that the means given to the state to fulfill its assignment is civil law with its punishments and rewards, set up and used according to the

light of reason (Romans 13:4). The light of reason includes the natural knowledge of God, the natural knowledge of the law, and conscience.

4. We believe the proper relation is preserved between the church and the state only when each remains within its divinely assigned sphere and uses its divinely entrusted means. The church should not exercise civil authority nor interfere with the state as the state carries out its responsibilities. The state should not become a messenger of the gospel nor interfere with the church in its preaching mission. The church should not attempt to use the civil law and force to lead people to Christ. The state should not seek to govern by means of the gospel. On the other hand, the church and the state may cooperate in an endeavor as long as each remains within its assigned place and uses its entrusted means.

5. We believe that Christians are citizens of both realms and serve God by faithfully fulfilling their duties in both (Romans 13:6,7).

6. We reject any attempt by the state to restrict the free exercise of religion.

7. We reject any views that look to the church to guide and influence the state directly in the conduct of its affairs.

8. We reject any attempt on the part of the church to seek the financial assistance of the state in carrying out its saving purpose.

9. We reject any views that hold that citizens are free to disobey such laws of the state with which they disagree on the basis of personal judgment.

This is what Scripture teaches about church and state. This we believe, teach, and confess.

IX. JESUS' RETURN AND THE JUDGMENT

1. We believe that Jesus, true God and true man, who rose from death and ascended to the right hand of the Father, will come again. He will return visibly, in the same way as his disciples saw him go into heaven (Acts 1:11).

2. We believe that no one can know the exact time of Jesus' return. This knowledge is hidden even from the angels in heaven (Matthew 24:36). Nevertheless, our Lord has given signs to his believers to keep them in constant expectation of his return (Matthew 24:4-14). He has told them to be alert and to watch so that day will not come upon them unexpectedly (Luke 21:34).

3. We believe that at Jesus' return this present world will come to an end. "In keeping with his promise we are looking forward to a new heaven and a new earth, the home of righteousness" (2 Peter 3:13).

4. We believe that when Jesus returns and his voice is heard throughout the earth, all the dead will rise, that is, their souls will be reunited with their bodies (John 5:28,29). Together with those still living, the resurrected will appear before his throne of judgment. The unbelievers will be condemned to an eternity in hell. Those who by faith have been cleansed in the blood of Christ will be glorified and will live with Jesus forever in the blessed presence of God in heaven (Philippians 3:21).

5. We reject the teaching that Christ will reign on earth for a thousand years in a physical, earthly kingdom.

This teaching (millennialism) has no valid scriptural basis and falsely leads Christians to set their hopes upon an earthly kingdom of Christ (John 18:36). We reject as unscriptural any claim that Christians will be physically removed, or "raptured," from the earth prior to judgment day. We likewise reject as unscriptural any claim that all the Jews will be converted in the final days.

6. We reject the teaching that Christians should look for one individual to arise in the end times as the great Antichrist. The characteristics of the Antichrist as presented in Scripture have been and are being fulfilled in the institution of the papacy (2 Thessalonians 2:4-10). We reject the opinion that the identification of the papacy with the Antichrist was merely a historical judgment valid only at the time of the Reformation.

7. We reject any denial of a bodily resurrection and of the reality and eternity of hell. We reject the teaching that the souls of people who have died return to earth in other bodies (reincarnation) (Hebrews 9:27).

8. We reject all attempts to interpret the New Testament descriptions of Jesus' second coming, of the end of the world, and of the judgment as mere figures of speech for events that take place not at the end of time but within the ongoing history of the world.

This is what Scripture teaches about Jesus' return and the judgment. This we believe, teach, and confess.